W9-CYA-424

The Dominie Collection of Traditional Tales
For Young Readers

The Princess & the Pea

Retold by Alan Trussell-Cullen

Illustrated by Elizabeth Sawyer

Dominie Press, Inc.

Once upon a time, there was a prince who wanted to marry a princess. But she had to be a *real* princess. So the prince traveled around the world, looking for a real princess.

He met many women who *looked like* princesses, but they weren't real princesses.

He met many women who *said* they were princesses, but they weren't real princesses.

So the prince went back home again.

One night there was a terrible storm. There was thunder and lightning. Sheets of rain poured down onto the castle.

In the middle of the storm there was a knock at the castle gate. The king himself went to see who was there.

The king opened the gate, and there before him stood a
princess. She said she was a *real* princess. But she was
wet from head to toe.

"You must come in and stay the night," said the king.

"We shall soon see whether she is a *real* princess or not," said the queen. And she made up a special bed for the princess.

First the queen laid a pea on the bed. Then she placed twenty mattresses on top of the pea. Then she placed twenty feather beds on top of the mattresses.

The princess was tired, so she went straight to bed.

In the morning, the queen asked the princess how she had slept.

"Terribly!" said the princess. "There seemed to be something hard in the bed. I tossed and turned all night!"

The queen was delighted. "Only a real princess would feel a pea through twenty mattresses and twenty feather beds!" she said.

The prince was delighted, too. He married the princess, and they lived happily ever after.